IN RECITAL®
WITH *Timeless Hymns*
(IN A CONTEMPORARY SETTING)

ABOUT THE SERIES • A NOTE TO THE TEACHER

In Recital® with Timeless Hymns is devoted to everlasting hymns that have been sung and heard throughout many generations. The outstanding arrangers of this series have created engaging arrangements of these hymns, which have been carefully leveled to ensure success. We know that to motivate, the teacher must challenge the student with attainable goals. This series makes that possible while also providing peaceful and joyous musical settings for your students. You will find favorites that are easy to sing along with, as well as recital-style arrangements. This series complements other FJH publications, and will help you plan student performances throughout the years. The books include CDs with complete performances designed to assist with performance preparation as well as for pure listening pleasure. Throughout this series you will find interesting background information for the hymns by Lyndell Leatherman.

Use the enclosed CD as a teaching and motivational tool. For a guide to listening to the CD, turn to page 43.

THE FJH MUSIC COMPANY INC.
Frank J. Hackinson

Production: Frank J. Hackinson
Production Coordinators: Joyce Loke and Satish Bhakta
Cover Design: Terpstra Design, San Francisco, CA
Cover Illustration: Keith Alexander
Engraving: Tempo Music Press, Inc.
Printer: Tempo Music Press, Inc.

ISBN-13: 978-1-56939-924-8

ORGANIZATION OF THE SERIES
IN RECITAL® WITH TIMELESS HYMNS

The series is carefully leveled into the following six categories: Early Elementary, Elementary, Late Elementary, Early Intermediate, Intermediate, and Late Intermediate. Each of the works has been selected for its artistic as well as its pedagogical merit.

Book Four — Early Intermediate, reinforces the following concepts:

- Students play pieces with common time signatures as well as compound meters.

- Students play pieces with more intricate finger crossovers.

- Students learn to play pieces with changes of tempo and articulations, and use the pedal.

- Major, minor, root position chords, and their inversions are reinforced, as well as subdominant, dominant, and major seventh chords.

- Left-hand parts increase in intricacy with more involved accompanimental figures and *ostinato* patterns. Two voices at the same time are sometimes played in the right hand.

- Hand positions expand larger than a fifth.

- Keys of C major, G major, F major, and D major.

Let Us Break Bread Together was arranged as an equal-part duet.
The rest of the selections are solos.

TABLE OF CONTENTS

ABOUT THE PIECES AND COMPOSERS

Sweet Hour of Prayer

Everyone who lived in Coleshill, England knew William W. Walford (1772-1850). During the week he sat in his trinket shop, carving novelties and decorations from ivory and old bones. His humble storefront was a favorite meeting place for the townsfolk, for though he had experienced more than his share of troubles in life, his cheerful outlook seem to lift the spirits of all who came in contact with him.

One day the local Congregational minister, Thomas Salmon, stopped by Walford's shop for his usual visit. The old shopkeeper, now seventy years of age, mentioned that he had composed a poem and wondered if the preacher would write the words down for him. Salmon gladly agreed to do so. Seventeen years later the text came to the attention of William B. Bradbury, a famous New York organist, choir director, composer, and compiler of sixty hymnbooks. Immediately he saw in Walford's text the potential for a popular hymn, and so he set it to music and included it in his next songbook, *Cottage Melodies*. Unfortunately, the kind old carver had died eleven years earlier, and so he never saw the wonderful response to his effort. In fact, Walford didn't see anything, and that's why he had asked the minister to write down the lyrics for *Sweet Hour of Prayer*—he was totally blind!

Jesus, Savior, Pilot Me

In 1870, Edward Hopper became pastor of a small chapel known as the Church of Sea and Land. Located close to the New York harbor, this church was attended mainly by men of the sea—sailors, fishermen, and their families. While there, Hopper learned all about ships and was inspired to write the lyrics *Jesus, Savior, Pilot Me*. Sailors in his congregation understood the song well—they knew all about charts, compasses, and the need for an expert pilot to guide ships around dangerous rocks and avoid collisions with other vessels. Hopper may have been inspired by the stories of Jesus calming the Sea of Galilee. He also have been inspired by the famous painting that shows Jesus standing behind the pilot of a ship guiding him to safety during a storm.

Sweet By and By

Sanford F. Bennett (1836-1898) was a Wisconsin doctor who wrote poetry as a hobby. One of his best friends was Joseph Webster (1819-1875), a local musician who was often depressed. Webster had been born and raised on the east coast, where he had written many popular songs. After moving to Wisconsin, he and Dr. Bennet began writing songs together. The doctor had learned to read his friend's moods, and often was able to bring him out of his blues by giving him a new text that needed a musical setting. One day Webster dropped in on Bennett at his office. Seeing Webster's sad look, Bennett asked, "What's the trouble now?" The musician replied, "It doesn't matter. Everything will be all right by and by." Bennett sat down immediately at his desk, and quickly wrote the three stanzas and refrain of *Sweet By and By* exactly as they are known today. While Bennett was writing, two other townsmen joined Webster around the stove and came up with the melody and harmony. In only half an hour, the hymn was finished. Playing the melody through on his violin, Webster taught it to the men in the office, and soon they were singing it in four-part harmony. It was first published in a collection titled *The Signet Ring,* and from there it spread quickly around the world.

O Worship the King

In 1785, Robert Grant was born into a wealthy and influential family in Scotland. His father, a director of the East India Company, was also a member of the British Parliament. After graduating from Cambridge University in 1806, Robert practiced law for twenty years and then was elected to Parliament. There, one of his great accomplishments was the introduction of a bill to remove restrictions placed on the Jews who were living in Great Britain. A deeply spiritual man, Grant wrote several hymns, all of which had careful craftsmanship and colorful imagery. His classic text *O Worship the King* is a paraphrase of Psalm 104.

Grant was later named Governor of Bombay in India, and it was there that he died four years later, in 1838, at the age of fifty-three.

This Little Light of Mine

This popular children's song was inspired by three verses from Jesus' Sermon on the Mount (Matthew 5:14-16). Jesus teaches us that we are the light of the world and should shine, just as a city that is set on a hill cannot be hidden. When people light a candle, they do not put it under a bushel, but on a candlestick, where it gives light to all that are in the house. He urges us to let our light shine before all so that they may see our good works and give glory to our Father who is in heaven.

What a Friend We Have in Jesus

The story behind *What a Friend We Have in Jesus* is both sad and inspiring. Its author, Joseph Scriven, was born in Dublin, Ireland in 1820 and spent several years in a military college. When poor health kept him from pursuing that goal further he took up theology, studying for the Anglican ministry. Then the night before he was to be married, his fiancée drowned in a freak accident—she was thrown from a horse into a river. Scriven then immigrated to Canada where, after some time, he fell in love again. But in another cruel twist of fate, his second fiancée died of pneumonia shortly after being baptized in a freezing cold lake. By most accounts, Scriven wrote his famous poem at this time, in 1857. Thirteen years later it was set to music by Charles C. Converse, an American lawyer and inventor who had studied classical music in Germany. The hymn was included in a collection titled *Gospel Hymns No. 1,* and soon became very popular around the world.

Scriven never married, nor did he get rich from the success of his hymn. He spent the rest of his life doing some tutoring, but mostly menial labor—mainly handyman work for widows and others too poor to hire help. Even though many thought he was rather sad and a bit strange, he was also known for a deep Christian faith that was demonstrated by the way he gave of his time and meager possessions to those in need.

Sweet Hour of Prayer

Music by William B. Bradbury
Lyrics by William Walford
arr. Edwin McLean

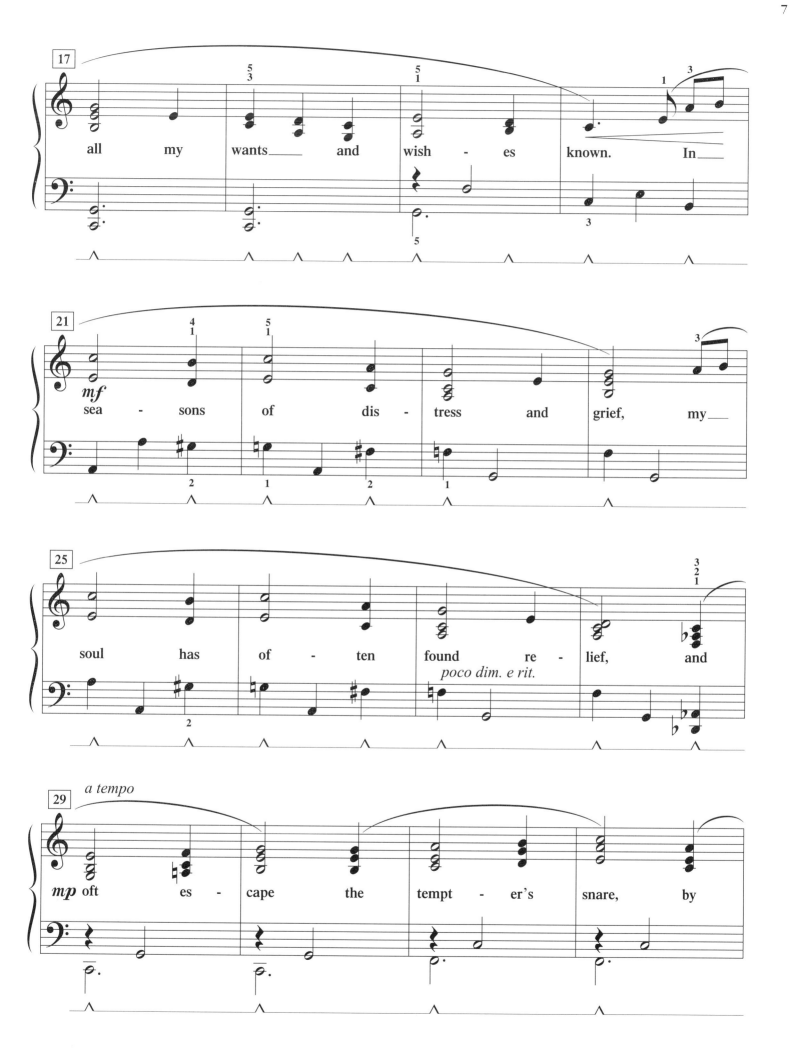

Jesus, Savior, Pilot Me

Music by John E. Gould
Lyrics by Edward Hopper
arr. Valerie Roth Roubos

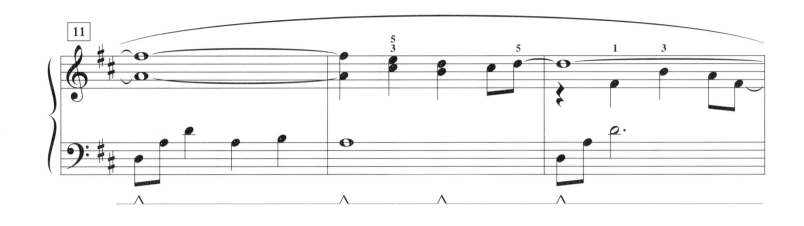

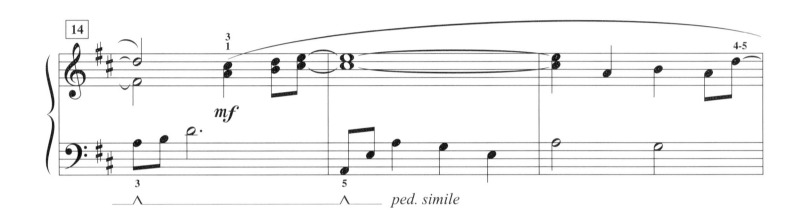

molto rit.

p

Sweet By and By

Music by Joseph P. Webster
Lyrics by Sanford F. Bennett
arr. Edwin McLean

O Worship the King

Music att. to Michael Haydn
Lyrics by Robert Grant
arr. Valerie Roth Roubos

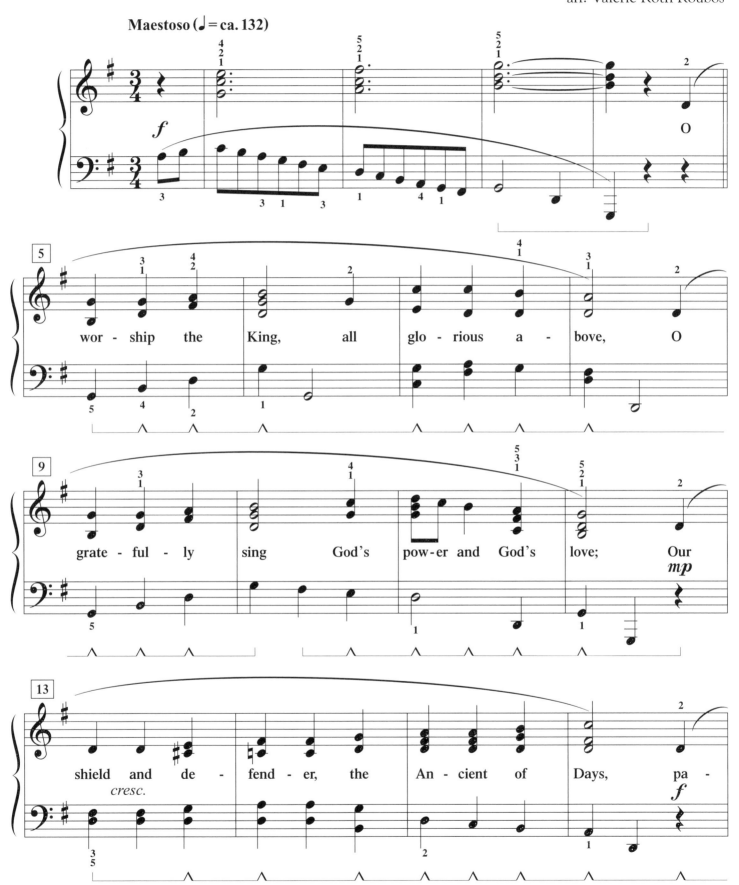

vil - ioned   in   splen - dor,   and   gird - ed   with

praise.

cresc.

ff

This Little Light of Mine

African-American Spiritual
arr. Nancy Lau

What a Friend We Have in Jesus

Music by Charles C. Converse
Lyrics by Joseph M. Scriven
arr. Robert Schultz

A Mighty Fortress Is Our God

Martin Luther
Lyrics trans. by Frederick H. Hedge
arr. Edwin McLean

Rejoice, the Lord Is King

Music by John Darwall
Lyrics by Charles Wesley
arr. Nancy Lau

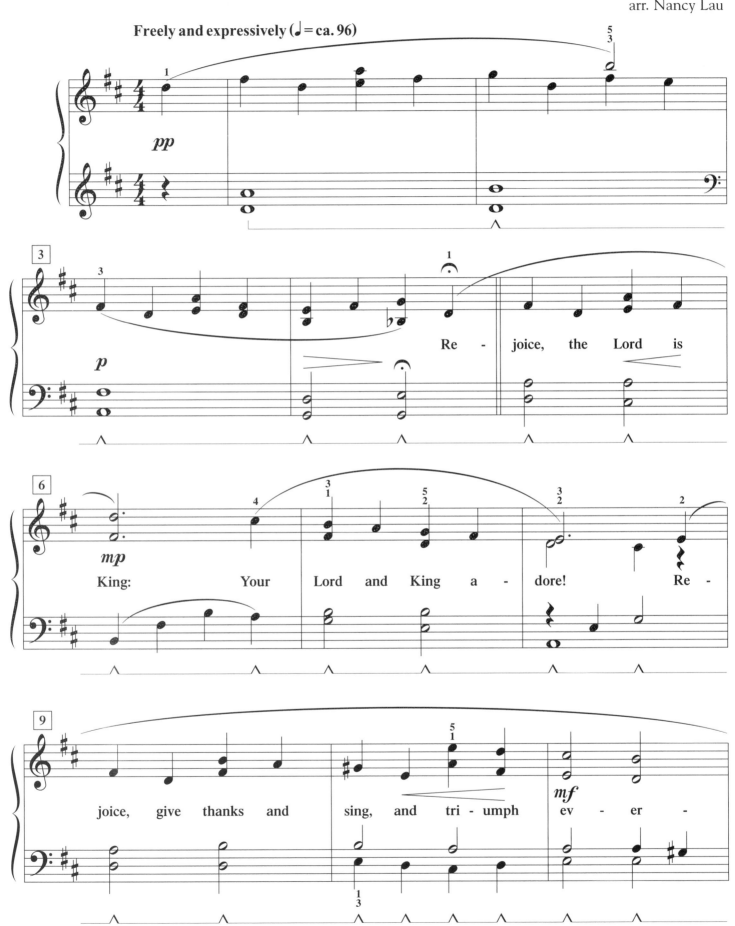

We Shall Overcome

African-American Spiritual
arr. Valerie Roth Roubos

Come, Thou Fount of Every Blessing

Music from John Wyeth's *Repository of Sacred Music, Part Second*
Lyrics by Robert Robinson
arr. Kevin Olson

Fervently, in a simple folk style (♩ = ca. 88)

30

FJH2145

Let Us Break Bread Together

Secondo

African-American Spiritual
arr. Edwin McLean

Let Us Break Bread Together

Primo

African-American Spiritual
arr. Edwin McLean

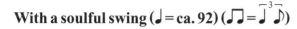

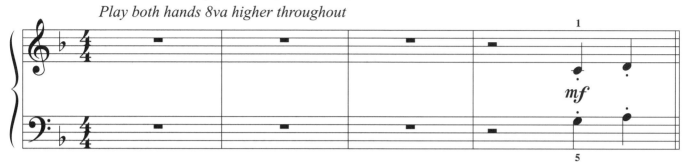

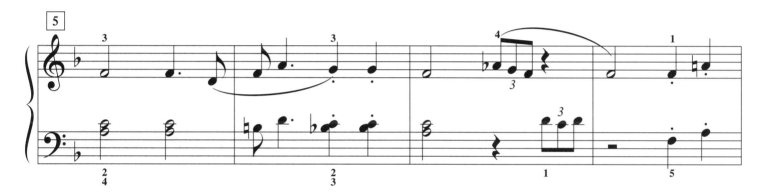

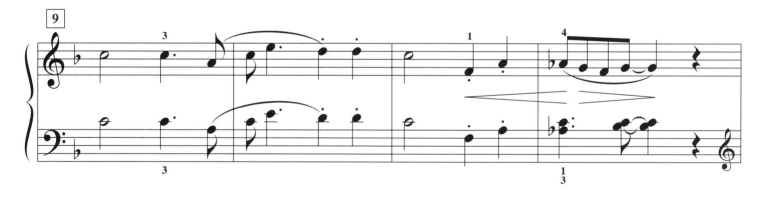

FJH2145

34

Secondo

FJH2145

Primo

Blessed Assurance

Music by Phoebe P. Knapp
Lyrics by Fanny J. Crosby
arr. Robert Schultz

ry, this is my song, prais - ing my Sav - ior all the day

long; this is my sto - ry, this is my song, prais - ing my

Sav - ior all the day long.

mp

FJH2145

ABOUT THE PIECES AND COMPOSERS

A Mighty Fortress Is Our God

In 1517, a German monk, Martin Luther, nailed a document to the door of the Wittenberg Castle Church in which he debated a religious issue of that day. The leaders of the church so strongly disagreed with him that they told him he had to leave—not only the church, but also his home. So he moved far away and spent his time praying, thinking, and writing. When he returned home four years later, he organized what came to be known as the Protestant Reformation, which gave people more choices of where to attend church.

At that time all the music in church was sung in Latin, which was considered to be the only language suitable for worshipping God. Luther thought that people in church should be able to sing in their own language (German, in this case). So he asked some of his friends to write some German hymns. But because that was such a new idea and everyone was so used to singing the same Latin chants over and over, his friends were slow to come up with anything. So Luther decided to try it himself. In all, he is thought to have written thirty-eight hymns. All have been forgotten except for one: *Ein' Feste Burg*—based on Psalm 34, and later translated as *A Mighty Fortress Is Our God*. This hymn spread like wildfire throughout Germany, then around the world. It has been translated into 184 different languages!

Rejoice, the Lord Is King

Charles Wesley (1707-1788) and his brother, John (1703-1791), both trained for ministry at Oxford University. Some other students jokingly called them "methodists" because of their strict schedule (or method) of religious exercises and study habits. After a short unsuccessful trip as missionaries to the American Colonies—Georgia, specifically—they returned home to England, frustrated in their spiritual lives. It was during the sea voyage back to England that spiritual seeds were planted in their hearts as they watched a group of Moravians experiencing amazing peace during a violent storm that threatened to sink their ship. The brothers soon experienced spiritual rebirth, and the rest is history, with John's preaching and Charles' hymn writing (over 6,500 hymn texts written in his lifetime!) starting a great revival that swept across England and became the foundation of the Methodist denomination.

We Shall Overcome

This melody is based on the tune of an old slave song. The original lyrics—from a song called *I'll Overcome Some Day*—were written around 1900 by Charles Tindley, an African-American minister who lived in Philadelphia. Through the years, both the melody and the lyrics kept changing as the song was passed along from singer to singer without being written down.

The hymn really became well known in the 1960s when Pete Seeger and Joan Baez, two folk singers, used it as the theme song of the civil rights movement in America. Since then its popularity has spread to many other countries, where it is sung by people longing for a world in which all are treated equally, no matter their color, gender, or economic status.

ABOUT THE PIECES AND COMPOSERS

Come, Thou Fount of Every Blessing

As a youth in London, Robert Robinson (1735-1790) was, by all accounts, destined for failure. Fatherless, he had joined a gang of troublemakers who roamed the streets. One night in 1752 their "agenda" included heckling a famous preacher, George Whitefield, who was speaking nearby. However, as the evangelist preached from the words of John the Baptist in Matthew 3:7: "O generation of snakes, who has warned you to flee from the judgment to come?" Robinson was reminded of his wickedness. That night he decided to turn his life around. Six years later, Robinson—now a pastor himself—wrote *Come, Thou Fount of Every Blessing* for the service of Pentecost at his church. A dizzying mixture of metaphors, it is quite possibly the only hymn to ever speak of raising an "Ebenezer"! (According to I Samuel 7:12, this was the name given to a stone monument honoring God's deliverance of His people, meaning literally, "stone of help.") Fifty-five years later and an ocean away, the text was first combined with the anonymous early-American tune that is most commonly associated with the hymn today—appearing in John Wyeth's *Repository of Sacred Music, Part Second*, published in 1813.

Let Us Break Bread Together

Some of the Africans who were brought to the American South on slave ships were very musical people. Sometimes they would pick up Bible stories or pieces of hymns and combine these words and melodies with their own songs. The slaves sang while laboring all day and then often met at night—sometimes secretly for fear of punishment— where they would improvise in song and dance for hours, even after a hard day's labor. These were songs of survival, songs that gave the courage to go on living when life seemed to be nothing but pain. Biblical stories such as Daniel in the lions' den, the Israelites' slavery in Egypt, and the birth of a Messiah—they all spoke powerful messages of hope to those who were oppressed. Sometimes their songs were created as a way of pouring out to God their deepest prayers, desires, and frustrations. *Let Us Break Bread Together* is one of these "spirituals"—as they became known— which is loved around the world. It was originally a "gathering song," used to announce an unauthorized meeting. When the traditional call to gather—a drumbeat—was outlawed in some southern states, this song served as a substitute, with a probable first stanza: "Let us praise God together..."

Blessed Assurance

Phoebe Palmer (1839-1908) was born in New York City, the daughter of a Methodist evangelist. She married Joseph Fairfield Knapp, a founder of the Metropolitan Life Insurance Company. She wrote more than 500 hymns and was widely respected as a hymn tune composer during her lifetime. On one occasion she visited her poetess friend, Fanny Crosby (1820-1915), and played this happy, lilting melody that she had recently composed. "What does the tune say?" she asked her host. Crosby didn't hesitate with her reply: "It says, 'Blessed assurance, Jesus is mine!' " Seizing the moment, Crosby went on to create the remaining text on the spot. This amazing lady, blind from birth because of a doctor's mistake, is thought to have written 8,000 hymn texts in her lifetime, many of which are still found in hymnals today. Rather than considering her blindness a handicap, she called it a blessing, saying, "When I get to heaven, the first face that shall ever gladden my sight will be that of my Savior."

ABOUT THE ARRANGERS

Nancy Lau

Nancy Lau (pronounced "Law") has often been told that her music sounds very lyrical and natural. She discovered her love and talent for music early in life. Born with perfect pitch, by age four Nancy was able to play nursery rhymes on the piano by ear. She was soon coming up with her own arrangements of songs and was able to copy any music that she heard.

An active composer, arranger, and piano teacher, Nancy studied music composition with Dr. Norman Weston and piano pedagogy with Nakyong Chai at Saddleback College in Orange County, California. In addition to writing for piano, she has composed for solo voice and chamber ensemble, and has written many choral works. Her compositions have won numerous awards. Nancy maintains a full piano studio, where her emphasis is on keeping music enjoyable and exciting. She believes that students must feel nurtured and accepted, and strives to generate in her piano lessons a joyful experience and positive memory.

Edwin McLean

Edwin McLean is a composer living in Chapel Hill, North Carolina. He is a graduate of the Yale School of Music, where he studied with Krzysztof Penderecki and Jacob Druckman. He also holds a master's degree in music theory and a bachelor's degree in piano performance from the University of Colorado.

Mr. McLean has authored over 200 publications for The FJH Music Company, ranging from *The FJH Classic Music Dictionary* to original works for pianists from beginner to advanced. His highly-acclaimed works for harpsichord have been performed internationally and are available on the Miami Bach Society recording, *Edwin McLean: Sonatas for 1, 2, and 3 Harpsichords*. His 2011 solo jazz piano album *Don't Say Goodbye* (CD1043) includes many of his advanced works for piano published by FJH.

Edwin McLean began his career as a professional arranger. Currently, he is senior editor for The FJH Music Company Inc.

Kevin Olson

Kevin Olson is an active pianist, composer, and member of the piano faculty at Utah State University, where he teaches piano literature, pedagogy, and accompanying courses. In addition to his collegiate teaching responsibilities, Kevin directs the Utah State Youth Conservatory, which provides weekly group and private piano instruction to more than 200 pre-college community students. The National Association of Schools of Music has recently recognized the Conservatory as a model for pre-college piano instruction programs. Before teaching at Utah State, he was on the faculty at Elmhurst College near Chicago and Humboldt State University in northern California.

A native of Utah, Kevin began composing at age five. When he was twelve, his composition, *An American Trainride*, received the Overall First Prize at the 1983 National PTA Convention at Albuquerque, New Mexico. Since then he has been a Composer in Residence at the National Conference on Piano Pedagogy, and has written music commissioned and performed by groups such as the American Piano Quartet, Chicago a cappella, the Rich Matteson Jazz Festival, and several piano teacher associations around the country.

Kevin maintains a large piano studio, teaching students of a variety of ages and abilities. Many of the needs of his own piano students have inspired more than 100 books and solos published by the FJH Music Company, which he joined as a writer in 1994.

ABOUT THE ARRANGERS

Valerie Roth Roubos

Valerie Roth Roubos earned degrees in music theory, composition, and flute performance from the University of Wyoming. Ms. Roubos maintains a studio in her home in Spokane, Washington, where she teaches flute, piano, and composition.

Active as a performer, adjudicator, lecturer, and accompanist, Ms. Roubos has lectured and taught master classes at the Washington State Music Teachers Conference, Holy Names Music Camp, and the Spokane and Tri-Cities chapters of Washington State Music Teachers Association. She has played an active role in the Spokane Music Teachers Association and WSMTA.

In 2001, the South Dakota Music Teachers Association selected Ms. Roubos as Composer of the Year, and with MTNA commissioned her to write *An American Portrait: Scenes from the Great Plains*, published by The FJH Music Company Inc. Ms. Roubos was chosen to be the 2004–2005 composer-in-residence at Washington State University. In 2006, WSMTA selected her as Composer of the Year. Ms. Roubos' teaching philosophy and compositions reflect her belief that all students, from elementary to advanced, are capable of musical playing that incorporates sensitivity and expression. Her compositions represent a variety of musical styles, including sacred, choral, and educational piano works.

Robert Schultz

Robert Schultz, composer, arranger, and editor, has achieved international fame during his career in the music publishing industry. The Schultz Piano Library, established in 1980, has included more than 500 publications of classical works, popular arrangements, and Schultz's original compositions in editions for pianists of every level from the beginner through the concert artist. In addition to his extensive library of published piano works, Schultz's output includes original orchestral works, chamber music, works for solo instruments, and vocal music.

Schultz has presented his published editions at workshops, clinics, and convention showcases throughout the United States and Canada. He is a long-standing member of ASCAP and has served as president of the Miami Music Teachers Association. Mr. Schultz's original piano compositions and transcriptions are featured on the compact disc recordings *Visions of Dunbar* and *Tina Faigen Plays Piano Transcriptions*, released on the ACA Digital label and available worldwide. His published original works for concert artists are noted in Maurice Hinson's *Guide to the Pianist's Repertoire, Third Edition*. He currently devotes his full time to composing and arranging. In-depth information about Robert Schultz and The Schultz Piano Library is available at the Website www.schultzmusic.com.

Using the CD

A great way to prepare for your recitals is to listen to the CD.

Enjoy listening to these wonderful pieces anywhere anytime! Listen to them casually (as background music) and attentively. After you have listened to the CD you might discuss interpretation with your teacher and follow along with your score as you listen.

Hymn Performances

Hymns	Where Played	Date	Special Memory of the Event
Sweet Hour of Prayer			
Jesus, Savior, Pilot Me			
Sweet By and By			
O Worship the King			
This Little Light of Mine			
What a Friend We Have in Jesus			
A Mighty Fortress Is Our God			
Rejoice, the Lord Is King			
We Shall Overcome			
Come, Thou Fount of Every Blessing			
Let Us Break Bread Together			
Blessed Assurance